Parenting:
The Bottom Line

RON MACKEY

Order this book online at www.trafford.com
or email orders@trafford.com

Most Trafford titles are also available at major online book retailers.

Printed in the United States of America.

ISBN: 978-1-4269-5520-4 (sc)
ISBN: 978-1-4269-5521-1 (hc)
ISBN: 978-1-4269-5522-8 (e)

Library of Congress Control Number: 2011900564

Trafford rev. 01/26/2011

www.trafford.com

North America & international
toll-free: 1 888 232 4444 (USA & Canada)
phone: 250 383 6864 • fax: 812 355 4082

Parenting : The Bottom Line

Little Tommy entered the local supermarket with his mother. She placed him in the grocery cart, and they began their journey down each aisle. Things were going well, she thought, but as she turned down the aisle with the candy and sweets she encountered a problem with her darling son.

He began to beg for some of the familiar sweets that he saw in the bright and colorful wrapping. But during the previous week, Mom and Tommy paid a visit to the dentist, who found far too many cavities in Tommy's teeth. So, Mom decided that Tommy could no longer have his favorite treats.

Now, that was not what her son wanted to hear. So, he began screaming at a high pitch, and throwing a temper tantrum. There was no doubt that Tommy's loud crying and screaming could be heard throughout the entire supermarket.

So, what was this young mother to do? What were her options? She could simply ignore her son's bad behavior, as many parents do in today's society. She could take him to the restroom and negotiate with him to calm down, because he was embarrassing her. She could just give in and buy him the candy and be done with his tantrum. But that would show him that his tantrum won him another victory over mean mommy. Another option she had was to get his attention with a swift pat on his back side. But wouldn't that type of response get her arrested for child abuse?

So, in order to avoid any further embarrassment, she decided to forego her grocery shopping trip for the day. She left all her groceries in the cart and departed the store to wait for a better time to come back and shop alone.

As I thought about that days' encounter, the first questions that came to my mind was, who was in charge, the child or the mother? And if she had the belief that she could be arrested for spanking her child for the purpose of correcting his behavior, was she correct in her thinking?

It had been stated by Lawrence Kutner, Ph.D, "that spanking simply does not work as a disciplinary technique". Well, I do not agree with his assessment. I believe that there are times when talking can be used as a tool for correcting the behavior of children,

And other times sending the little ones to there room without the television, I-Pod, videos, or any form of entertainment could possibly get your point across. But when all the other methods of discipline fail, nothing else gets their attention like a few swats on the "old seat of understanding".

The subject of spanking, as a means of parental discipline, has sparked much controversy over recent years. And I have read about many people, including doctors, psychologists, and child development specialists, espousing the notion that the spanking of children leads to the likelihood of violent behavior in later years.

Dr. Katherine Jones, a clinical psychologist in Alabama, "stated that even Black parents have become "softer" when it comes to disciplining their children. She once commented that "one of the primary problems with parents is that they are more "self-absorbed" in their careers and individual needs.

She went on to say that "parents don't have a lot of time for parenting and attending to their children as they had in the past". Now, I truly agree with her insight. I see it every day.

When a child gets in trouble at school, some parents don't make time to go the school and meet with the teachers to see what the problems are with their children. Nor even bother to attend local PTA meetings. And those types of parents get angry with the teachers for bothering them, and wasting their time about their children.

I believe that such actions by some parents is a form of neglect, and is in essence child abuse. Every child that is born into this world deserves special care and protection from their parents, and whether parents realize it or not, love, guidance, correction, and discipline are a very important part of the responsibility of being a parent.

Parents need to understand that parent-teacher conferences are a very important part in a child's life, in that it allows the parents and teachers to work together in order to help a student learn and be successful.

And meeting the student's teacher and understanding classroom rules and expectations is a benefit for the parents and students. And if the parents know the rules of the classroom and the educational expectations, they will be able to enforce those expectations at home and help their child better adjust to those expectations.

Dr. Jones also stated that "many parents run their households as if it was a democracy, where everyone in the house has an equal say, including the children". And that to me is definitely not an appropriate way to run a household. Parents need to firmly establish themselves as adults and head of the household, but they tend to let things slip.

If the things that Dr. Jones spoke about were fully established in the home, we would not have half of the crime in this nation that we currently have. In today's society, parents need to be parents, and not only take responsibility for the actions of the children, but hold their children accountable for their own actions.

Dr. Jerry Collins, a clinical neurophysiologist in California, wondered, "if discipline was a dying art that parents no longer demanded in children?" He believed that, "instilling discipline in children teaches them about family matters and other important factors in life, such as the meaning of boundaries, and what is acceptable and unacceptable behavior in our society."

Dr. Collins also pointed out that "the majority of single-parent households in the Black community are headed by women, and those families often lack a suitable male role model, and consequently, life for most Black males and for many qrown men is a frustrating search for the lost father who has not yet offered protection, provisions, nurturing, modeling, and especially love."

According to 2000 Census data, in certain zip codes in inner city Baltimore, Maryland, over 95 percent of the children are raised in single-parent homes. And for all intents and purposes, marriage as a cultural institution in those areas was extinct, and the government played a large role in killing it with the Great Society welfare solutions of the 1960's.

Those programs that were designed to be helpful took away the responsibility of the father to provide for his children, and placed the responsibility on the mother, and the government took on the role of the father. And many families have suffered great consequences because of it.

Dr. Collins notes an excerpt from a book written by Erich Fromm entitled " The Art Of Loving", and in it he observed that, " a father's love is conditional on how well the child obeys his wishes, and how well he achieves something of significance to the father." "It is, he says, a father's love that motivates the child to obey the laws of a society, and to adopt its values.

He also observed that, "teenagers mostly supervise themselves today, than ever before." And he recalled the words of a 14-year-old in one of his counseling sessions as saying, "my parents let me do anything I want to do as long as I don't get into trouble."

Now, in my own experience, I can recall several instances in my childhood where I chose to bypass known limitations and boundaries set by my parents in a stand of rebellion. I realized in those instances, that I disappointed my parents, as well as exhibited a lack of respect for them by my errant behavior.

I will say that it did not take long for my father to relay the message to my "seat of understanding" that such behavior was not acceptable, and would not be tolerated in the future, and to me the message was clear.

After I realized the error of my ways, I apologized for my misbehavior, got a hug from my parents and went out to play, realizing that I had parents who loved me, and were willing to do as responsible parents have a duty and a responsibility to do, and that is to love, guide, nurture, correct and protect their children, and help them to grow up to become productive adult citizens.

Many child psychologists often warn that spanking slows mental development and hinders achievement. And other opponents of spanking make claims that when spanking is used as a disciplinary measure, it causes irreparable harm to children and effects them mentally and physically later in their adult life.

Now, in my research, I ran across an article by Del Jones, of USA Today, entitled, "Top CEO's were spanked as kids. Does spanking make a difference?" The article reported that, "of the 20 CEO's Del Interviewed, all of them were spanked as children.

"He talked about how the debate over spanking remains unresolved, but there is one thing the CEO's overwhelmingly had in common. As children, they were paddled, belted, switched or swatted." As the article continued, "those CEO's were interviewed for over three months and while none said they were abused, neither were any spared."

Del reported that "typical is General Motors (GM) CEO Rick Wagoner, who got an occasional "whack on the fanny," while growing up in Richmond, Virginia, but said, "he had it coming, and that it probably had no influence on his life as a high achiever."

Further in the article, the question is asked, "is spanking what caused the eventual success of these CEO's" The answer is, probably not, but something more important needed to be understood. If a parent wants their child to grow up and be successful at life (not just work, but relationships as well) then whether they choose to spank, or give time-outs, the key is consistent, and loving discipline.

But, as I observe today's society, I see a great neglect taking place in the area of parental guidance, and discipline. Many children today are not taught by parents to say "Yes Sir, and No Maam," when acting in response to adults and elderly people. "Yeah, and No" seem to be sufficient responses toward adults by many of today's children and youth.

It seems to me, that many children and youth have an ultimate disrespect for their parents and other adults and have no idea what discipline is. Could it be because parents are afraid that they may get arrested for even raising their voices at their children.

I have no doubt that these children need more discipline and guidance than what they are getting now, as opposed to "easy" parents giving in to them at every turn.

I don't know if you realize it, but kids are pretty smart today, and they know how to play their parents to the maximum degree. And they will do it as long as they can get away with it. Most parents and grandparents realize that children do not come from the womb knowing the difference between right and wrong. So knowing that fact, it must be understood by all parents, that children need to be taught what is acceptable and unacceptable behavior in the home and in society.

They must also be taught in their young lives to meet the expectations you have set for them and that you expect good behavior from them most of the time, and if you take the time to do it, and live by example, they will understand.

At times people often equate discipline with punishment. Now the word discipline is defined as the practice, or methods of teaching and enforcing acceptable patterns of behavior. And the reason parents need to discipline and train their children is to teach them to acquire a sense of self-control that they can practice as they grow to adulthood.

My wife and I made this nurturing process a part of our lives in raising our daughter. And now we see that same nurturing process taking place in her family today. Now, when it comes to parental guidance, most people wish that an instruction manual came with every newborn, but many parents don't realize that there is a parental instruction manual found in the Bible, and I believe that it prescribes adequate instruction concerning the raising and discipline of children. And when it comes to the discipline of children, the Bible prescribes the following passage which states, "He who spares the rod hates his son, but he who loves him is diligent to discipline him." (Proverbs 13:24, King James Version, (KJV).

And another passage concerning the raising, and guidance of children is found in Proverbs 22:15 reads this way; "Foolishness is bound up in the heart of a child, but the rod of correction will drive it far from him." New King James Version, (NKJV).

I believe that the Creator of the universe knows better about parenting than any human on this earth could ever learn, and our Heavenly Father placed these guidelines in the Bible to help earthly parents in the raising of their offspring.

Now, everyone would agree that many parents are having a hard time with their children and are at their wits end, wishing that their children would just go away. But, if they would simply follow divine counsel from God's Word concerning the raising and guidance of children, their lives would be much better.

One way that we can show love to our children is to follow the counsel of Proverbs 22:6, which reads, "Train up a child the way he should go; and when he is old, he will not depart from it." (KJV). And this includes teaching our children the difference between right and wrong.

Parents must be aware that God holds them accountable for their children, and that means that parents are to nurture, instruct, correct and discipline their children. One other interesting text that I found to be very clear on the subject of parenting is in Proverbs 19:18, which reads, "Chasten thy son while there is hope, and let not thy soul spare for his crying." (KJV).

Now, if I understand this Bible texts correctly, parents are counseled to correct their children, when they practice misconduct. King Solomon seemed to be warning fathers not to neglect chastisement of the sons, lest the son's life come to ruin.

He is simply saying that early correction and punishment is proper, when it comes to children, because when a youth is set in his evil ways, there is less hope of reformation. Now, there is one more of many Bible texts that deal with the subject of children and discipline, and that is found in Proverbs 23:13-14, and it reads, "Withhold not correction from the child; for if thou beatest him with a rod, he shall not die". Thou shalt beat him with the rod, and shall deliver his soul from hell".

Now, there is one point that needs to be understood by all parents. There are many different disciplinary techniques that can be used to instill good behavior in children. And if spanking is one of the choices, it should only be used once all other avenues of disciplinary measures have not resolved the behavioral issue at hand.

But let there be a balance, and a consistency in parenting. And that means not being too strict, nor being too loose, but consistent. I say this because children must learn that the reason for correction is to get their attention, and to change the direction of their behavior.

And too often parents in today's society, postpone any kind of correction or discipline until their children are old enough to reason with; only to discover that they find themselves in the grip of habits of behavior that are so deep in their children, that those habits can hardly be broken.

In the light of this prescribed Bible counsel, it should not be the responsibility of the local restaurant owner, or the supermarket manager, to correct your children when they misbehave in those establishments. There was an article in the newspaper concerning a Chicago restaurant owner who placed a sign in his establishment.

On the sign was written the words; "CHILDREN OF ALL AGES HAVE TO BEHAVE, AND USE THEIR INDOOR VOICES." This came after the children of some parents were using the radiator pipes to climb the walls, "Spiderman style", and the parents did nothing to correct them.

The owner said that when other customers came in and saw the misbehavior of those children they turned around and walked out. This caused him to remind parents to keep charge of their children when entering his establishment.

Surprisingly, the posting of that sign led to a boycott of his restaurant by angry parents. This is further evidence that it is the responsibility of parents to use whatever means necessary, to let their erring children know when their behavior is not acceptable, and when parents fail, it is time for the restaurant owners to take charge of the situation, to make their place of business a safe, and comfortable environment for a family to be in.

It is very important for parents to discuss which disciplinary technique they will use for their child, and come to an agreement, even before the child is born. Or they will find that they have made a grave and deadly mistake by the time their child reaches the youth and teen stages of their lives, and that will be too late.

It is also important to understand that discipline and correction isn't something you enforce because you hate your children. You discipline and correct them because you love them.

I have been a school bus driver for over 22 years and I have come into contact with thousands of children of all ages. There have been instances when I have warned students about violations of the rules of conduct on the bus.

With those warnings, I have made each student aware that if they continue with the same misconduct, I would have no choice but to forward a written referral to the school administrator informing them of rule violations on the bus, and that same information would be forwarded to their parents, or guardians.

Now, in response to my informing the erring students of what would happen if I turned in the referrals, I was told by a number of students that it didn't matter if I wrote a referral on them, because their parents would not do anything to them anyway for their misconduct. And I find that response to be a sad commentary on parental discipline.

Now, in a number of conversations I have had with parents on the subject of spanking as a form of discipline, I have heard parents and grandparents say that all they had to do was talk with their children and grandchildren when they misbehaved, and they were able to correct errant behavior without any more difficulties.

Now, I applaud those parents who have set limitations and boundaries in their households, and have taken time to discuss, and choose how they would discipline their children. But there are many households that have no structure or rules in the home at all.

And the parents in those particular homes have no clue as to how to deal with erring children, and those are the households that have the most child abuse, due to a lack of parenting skills.

Thus, there are parents who have no idea how to raise and discipline a child, and when their child misbehaves, they respond by hitting them while angry and being in a fit of anger is not the proper time to discipline a child.

Many parents don't understand that different techniques can be used to correct children when they misbehave. Some parents can simply speak to their child with love, and let them know how disappointed they are at their child's conduct, and the problem is resolved with no further action, like the parents I spoke about earlier.

Other parents get their point across by removing certain privileges from their erring child, like the television, CD player, I-Pods, computer, and video games, if the child continues to disobey the house rules. Other parents use "time-outs," where a child is put in a corner, or a designated spot for a certain period of time, or sent to their bedroom, until they understand the error of their ways.

Then, there are other parents who just overlook whatever their children do. And it does not matter whether they are at home, or out in public. It is either through ignorance, or parents are just tired of trying to correct them, so they just give up and let them have their way.

This lack of parental discipline presents a very difficult situation for teachers who are trying to educate these out-of-control children. In a news article from April 25, 2005, elementary school teachers and their principal in Miami, Florida deemed a 5-year-old female so unruly in the classroom, that they called the police.

As the child was handcuffed and led from the building, she began a felonious plight arousing controversy. In the article, the question was asked, "Did a child's tantrum pose a threat worthy of the Miami Police Department?" It is sad to say, but out-of-control youngsters, and hapless adults (which are mostly parents) have become commonplace.

We do know that there is a parental disconnect with children in today's society when we see programs on television such as "SuperNanny", and "Nanny 911", Where modern day parents invite a professional Nanny into their home to set up parenting skills training, as well as communication programs for extremely dysfunctional families.

And I was really shocked, when on one of those segments, I saw five-year-old hitting and kicking his mother repeatedly during one of his uncontrollable temper tantrums, and all the mother could do was run into her bedroom, shut her door and cry. And that was not all. That five-year-old boy that she gave birth to, was outside her bedroom door kicking it numerous times, while yelling and screaming at her at the same time.

Now, some may say that the little boy could not control himself, because he was probably suffering from (ADD) Attention Deficit Disorder, or (ADHD) Attention Deficit Hyperactivity Disorder, which are development and behavioral disorders that affect 3 to 5 percent of all school-age children.

Now, I agree that one of these disorders could possibly be the cause of this five-year-olds problem., but (ADD) and (ADHD) has been the "diagnosis of choice" for many behavioral problems in children and youth for a number of years.

It has been suggested that over seventy-five percent of all children that have been evaluated for these, and similar disorders receive medication on the very first visit to the Doctor. Could it be that (ADD), and (ADHD) might be used in some situations as a cover for neglectful parenting?

Now please notice some of the symptoms in children diagnosed with these disorders: (1) Such children are easily distracted by sights and sounds in their environment. (2) They are unable to concentrate for long periods of time on low stimulation tasks such as sitting in class doing homework, and completing chores around the house. (3) These children have a tendency to daydream, and are slow to complete simple tasks.

But wait a yoctosecond! It appears to me, that the behaviors I just described could be diagnosed in almost any child on this planet earth. And if you look at the sales of video games, and track the amount of hours spent by children and youth watching movies on their DVD players; the hours spent watching T.V.; the hours spent listening to this "so-called music" on the I-PODS, I-Phones, and on most cell phones, I ask all of you a question.

Now, where is the deficit in their attention span when it comes to participating in those various forms of entertainment? Yet, those children exhibit a "deficit of attention" when it comes to misbehaving in class, doing homework after school; and doing chores around the house like cutting the grass, washing the dishes, and cleaning their rooms.

Even though many of these disorders are probably legitimate in some cases, could it be possible, that in a great majority of the diagnosed cases, and the drugs used to treat these disorders, are being sought by some parents to excuse errant behavior, and to cover up a "deficit in parenting"? And even though bad parenting may not cause (ADD), or (ADHD), it could possibly add to the impairment that these disorders cause.

Now, in my research, I have discovered a possible third disorder. It is not a disorder of the child, but a disorder suffered by the parent. It is a disorder called (NWTB), which stands for "Not Whipping That Butt"!

Now, parents who are suffering from the (NWTB) syndrome do not need any drugs to calm them down, or drugs to stimulate them, but they simply need to carry out their God-given parental responsibilities, and apply whatever disciplinary measures they have neglected to implement, if their child is ignoring repeated warnings, and especially if their child is clearly out-of-control in their behavior.

Another thing to consider. Are the parents not giving their child any attention? The children may be using bad behavior to get the attention that they desire. Have you heard the old saying, "negative attention is better than no attention at all?"

And if you have ever had the blessing of having a new born baby, you know that they demand maximum attention right from the first day they come into this world.

Now, there could be a slight possibility that little Tommy's mother might be suffering from that (NWTB) disorder as well as lacking the parenting skills needed to teach her child to understand what is acceptable and unacceptable behavior at home, and in public places.

Be it known that this subject is not talked about very much, but a larger part of the problem with so many out-of-control children, is that there are thousands of unwed mothers out there who have never been married, with one or more children who are in dire need of a father figure in the home.

Since one out of four babies in America are born to single mothers, this is one of the reasons for the high level of poverty being experienced in many cities in America. It is hard for me to understand, but it seems that single parenthood by choice has become very common-place in America. Perhaps it could be partly blamed on the more than 50% rate of divorce in the late 1960s; the increasing number of single-parent families; and the changes in public attitudes about a couple living together, which not makes single-parenthood itself no longer so stigmatizing,

So given these changes in attitude, a young woman who finds herself pregnant, and for whatever reason does not really want to marry the father, is in a totally different environment than in the past.

And research brings out the fact that over one-half of all single parent families now begin by an unmarried birth. It is also interesting to note that one-third of all children in the United States are now born to an unmarried mother. One-half of the fore-mentioned births are second or higher order births, and these are not just first births, and certainly not just teen births.

And it is reported that only a third of unmarried childbearing occurs to teens; which the majority of these births occur later in life. An article by Erik Eckholm in the New York Times on March 18, 2009, headlined that, "2007 U. S. Births Break Baby Boom Record". The article goes on to say that, "More babies were born in the United States in 2007 that in any other year in American history, according to preliminary data reported by Stephanie J. Ventura, chief of reproductive statistics at the National Center for Health Statistics".

It is an astounding fact that, "4,317,000 births just edged out the figure for 1957, at the height of the baby boom". She reported that, "the increase reflected a slight rise in childbearing those in their 30's and 40's, and a record share of births to unmarried women. She also stated that, "this growth in births has mainly been fueled by increases among adult women."

She also said that, "racial and ethnic differences remain large: 28 percent of white babies were born to unmarried mothers in 2007, compared to 51 percent of Hispanic babies, and 72 percent of Black babies." "And the shares of births to unwed mothers among Whites and Hispanics have climbed faster than the share among Blacks but from lower starting points."

So, this trend toward unmarried childbearing in the United States has not occurred primarily among minorities. Among Caucasian women in the United States at virtually every age, there has been an increase in the rate of unmarried childbearing. And there are comparable trends in Europe, Canada, Australia and New Zealand, and most obviously in Scandinavia.

And on this basis, we see that the significance of marriage for childbearing has clearly declined. The roots of all this can be found in delayed marriage and in the separation of sex from marriage.

It is important to mention that many of today's T.V. shows, and movies tend to promote the value of single-parenting, and "shacking up" as approved, and acceptable behavior in society. And, it is a well-known fact that the traditional two-parent family, with a father and a mother, brings stability and balance in all areas of family life, including the raising, nurturing and disciplining of children.

But these unwed and single-mothers are more than likely the only means of support for their children. If they work, they piece together two or three jobs to try to provide for themselves, and their children, which is by no means enough to live on. But I do have to say, that the laws are getting better as far as catching up with some of the "deadbeat sperm donors" who have no connection at all, with all of the thousands of children that they helped to bring into this world.

But, that does not change the situation of the children not having anyone at home to help feed, clothe, love and protect them. It is time for all of those "deadbeats" to step up to the plate, be real men, and take care of their financial responsibilities to their children, even if the mother and father don't care for each other.

With all of the talk on T.V. and radio every day about how many children live in poverty in America, it is not hard to trace the root causes of poverty and homelessness.

Many of the causes could be linked to the out-of-control, out-of-wedlock babies that are born to these young-and-still--getting-younger females, who are "used" by these young-and-still-getting-younger male "sperm donors", who have nothing else to offer these young females, except "I LOVE YOU." But, they forget to add, "until you get pregnant, then I don't know you."

So, what are the lives of many of these young unwed mothers like? These mothers who have no means of financial support are working so many hours that they don't have time to relax, or to even get a reasonable amount of sleep. And this means that they have no real quality time to spend with their children.

So, the real question is, Who is looking after the children while Mom is working? the answer is, some children are blessed to be able to stay with grandparents, uncles and aunts, cousins and other relatives, or family friends.

But so many children are left at day care centers for sometimes more than 24-hours, Some are simply left at home alone, because day care is quite expensive, especially if there is more than one child involved. So, there are many children left to themselves, and their only babysitter is the television, computer, and video games.

And if you really think about it, many of those same children who are between the ages of 8 and 13 years-old are easy pickings for gang recruiters, who were also more than likely, left home alone at that same age, with little or no supervision. So, the vicious cycle continues from generation to generation.

Now, it does not take a rocket scientist to come to the conclusion that children need a structured existence. And it is the parents responsibility to provide the structure and guidance needed to nurture their children from infancy to adulthood, and to teach them how to make right decisions throughout their lives.

In a February, 2003 article from the U.S. General Services Administration, the U.S. Census bureau stated that, "in the year 2000 there were over 4.5 million children (under 18 years of age) living in homes maintained by their grandparents". It went on to say that "the number of children raised in grandparent-headed households has increased by 30% since 1990." It continued, by stating, "while the majority of grandparents raising grandchildren are between ages 55 and 64, 20% to 25% are over age 65".

Now you may be asking why this is happening. Some of the reasons involve a single parent becoming overwhelmed with financial problems. The children's parents being incarcerated, succumbing to illnesses, substance abuse, or death. Other reasons are the high rate of divorce, teen pregnancies, and long deployments of parents in the military.

And it goes without saying that this puts an overwhelming burden on the grandparents who have spent all of their working lives raising their own children and preparing for retirement, and are faced with the stresses of raising another generation of children to adulthood. And if you are among this group of heroes and fine citizens I salute you, and being grandparents, my wife and I would do the same for our grandchild as well.

Now, many parents today are not aware of this, but there is a generational mindset that started in the late 1950's and early 1960's in the area of parenting, that set in motion a decline in the practice of parental guidance.

There were books that were written instructing parents to not be so strict on their children, and suggested the idea that loving care alone, instead of a disciplinarian approach to parenting.

When it came to the controversial issue of spanking in that era, parents did not realize that there was a right way, and a wrong way to spank. Now, when I speak of The wrong way to spank, that includes using extension cords; razor straps; tree limbs; and various kitchen utensils such as spatulas and large wooden spoons.

But, most of all, many parents of that day, executed their wrath on their children while in fits of anger for their child's misbehavior, and in their anger they more than likely caused bodily injury or even death to that child, which was in essence child abuse.

We must acknowledge that any extreme in parenting is not good, and there must be a balance. And most doctors and child psychologists of that time, focused so much on the wrong way of parenting, that parents revolted against correction of any kind being used, and this parental neglect resulted in losing control of their children.

John Rosemond, Ph.D, in his book, "To Spank Or Not To Spank", discussed issues associated with spanking children, as well as how to do it correctly. He stated several times in the book, "that he is not a proponent of spanking," but stated that "spanking a child, if it is done correctly, is not harmful to a child and is actually helpful.

Now, he suggested "four ways" to spank a child appropriately. In his first step he notes that "A child should be spanked only as a way to provide an immediate halt to an unacceptable behavior."

"It is a way to say "Stop and Listen!" to a child." Rosemond offered the analogy that "one, quick open-handed slap to the clothed bottom of a child, is to abuse, as sending a child to his room is, to locking a child in the closet."

"And of course either extreme is abuse, but at the "reasonable end " of the continuum, the need to halt the child's behavior is the same." He also notes that "spanking is not to humiliate a child. Spanking in public does that." Further, "when others are around to see the spanking, that child sees them and they distract the child from the message you are trying to give him or her."

The second step that Rosemond gives "is that spanking should be followed by a short explanation and a consequence ie, "You will not be allowed to speak to me or your father like that.

Now go to your room until dinner time." He adds that, "time outs; losing some privilege for the rest of the day; going to bed early, etc.... are also effective disciplinary tools.

Rosemond explains that, "with a toddler at the age of 24-months or so, a quick pat on the butt, followed by the reprimand (ie, "No, I will not let you spit at me," then the consequence is effective." "For a young child, placing the child in a chair with the warning, "you will stay there until I say you can get up"; followed by taking a step backward; waiting one second, and then telling the child, "Now, you can get up," is sufficient."

This catches the child's attention, provides a rule, provides a consequence, and establishes that you are in charge." Rosemond's third step suggests that "correction should quickly, and immediately follow the undesired behavior.

Repeated warnings, pleadings, and eventual "blowups" followed by spanking when the parent is out of control and angry, are not discipline, or correction, for they do not slow or halt the undesired behavior." He goes on to say that "correction does not necessarily include spanking." And he further argues that "the value of spanking is in it's novelty. If it is only used for immediately halting a child's out-of-control behavior on occasion, then the child will not get "used to it", and learn to ignore it."

Now, when the question is asked, how often should you spank? Rosemond says, "for young children, if it is more than once per week, it is likely too much. With older children once a month is probably OK. And with children over age 9 or 10, it is not effective."

Now, in the fourth and last step, Rosemond says that "effective spankings are not accompanied by yelling and name-calling. They are never motivated by rage. They can be motivated by anger, but the point of the anger is not to make the child feel threatened, frightened, or more hurt."

He states that "the point of anger is to mark the experience in the child's head, and to convey to them, " this crossed some line: this is serious". Rosemond emphasizes that everything is not serious, so again, spanking too often defeats the purpose of spanking at all.

Rosemond notes that "effective spanking is not a last resort. Spanking is only useful if it draws a child's attention to a problematic behavior and your decisions about it if it is done early, quickly, and without fuss. If a child has repeatedly disobeyed you, the problem is that you failed to set and hold limits."

He says that "if a child repeatedly disobeys after being warned once, spanked and punished, then the behavioral cycle is serious and spanking will not help at this point."

Now, the revolutionary "soft" parenting approach that I referred to earlier, had a huge impact on the way that most of the "baby boom" generation was raised. And in my opinion, it was that deadly infusion of secular idealogy about parenting, that set the stage for the permissive society that we have arrived at today.

And there is a whole generation of young people who are without discipline because of such ideology. Thus, the age-long Biblical position on parenting was replaced by a more permissive outlook. This brought forward a secular belief system of values without the Biblical foundation.

This secular belief system of values has had a major influence on our society, and it comes to us through the media of television, books, movies, video games and the world wide web.

Now, I submit to you, that any intelligent, and observant person can see that this media is very powerful in there liberal and permissive agenda, and the only possible way to avert these destructive influences of sex and violence on our young people is for parents is to stand up and take charge before their children are succumbed by this liberal and secular value system. And it is of the utmost importance for parents to be aware of where their children are at all times, and know what they are viewing in the media.

Now, there are parents in this country with a more relaxed and permissive outlook on parenting. They approve of providing alcohol and drugs for their teenager's parties, have the attitude that their teens are going to drink or do drugs anyway, so they as may as well do it at home, where it is safe.

And decisions such as that have very serious consequences. In an article written in June 2007 by Staff Writer Daniela Deane of the Washington Post "a mother and stepfather were serving 27-month jail sentences for serving alcohol to minors at a 16th birthday party for their son."

The article went on to say that "Elisa Kelly and George Robinson, now divorced, pleaded guilty to nine misdemeanor counts of contributing to the delinquency of a minor stemming from the backyard party for their son Ryan who is now in his early twenties."

Now, the parents who hosted the party bought beer and wine for their sons' friends with the understanding that they would stay the night. The mother collected the car keys to make sure that no one left the party. She also reasoned, as many parents do, that "the kids were going to drink regardless", and she wanted to keep them off of the road.

According to the article, the party came to an end as a result of police going to the home after receiving calls about underage drinking. When the police arrived they found about 30 young people, between 12 and 18 years of age running into the woods when someone yelled, "Cops!"

Now, just think how many times this scene takes place all over the country because parents fail to set a proper standard for their children to follow and hold them accountable when they don't.

Now, according to the 2007 National Highway Traffic Safety Administration (NHTSA) statistics, "there were approximately 13,041 people killed in alcohol-impaired driving accidents. and 1,719 of that number, were drivers between the ages of 16 thru 20 years-old."

This fact is one of many reasons for parents to talk openly to their children about alcohol use and abuse, and the many dangers that are associated with it. And if you do this early in their lives, you will possibly prevent much heartache and sorrow in your family and others as well.

And as you know, many teens are given a wide latitude in the use of alcohol and drugs in today's society, and if the parents are soft in that area, their teens will be given the same latitude when it comes to the area of sex.

So, the parents go a step further by providing their teenage sons with condoms, and their teenage daughters with a choice of condoms, or birth-control pills. And in the homes where this occurs, the subject of abstinence is never mentioned because of this more permissive attitude.

Now, what age should parents begin to set standards for their offspring to follow? Should parents start while the child is in infancy, or should they let things go until until the child is thirteen or fourteen years-old?

Everybody knows that a baby is not born with a wealth of knowledge when they come from the womb. So, they need to be taught from infancy to adulthood what is acceptable, and what is not acceptable behavior. The problem with many parents today is that they have never taught their children to understand the connection between actions and consequences.

These lessons begin with the parents because children learn attitudes from their parents. And if parents have a wrong attitude, their children will develop a wrong attitude as well. And we are all aquainted with the "terrible two's." Now, the "terrible two's don't have to be terrible, if the parents set the behavior pattern for their child.

Now, I can tell you that parents who follow a more "flexible", and "child-friendly" approach to parenting, such as allowing their children to call them by their first names instead of Mom and Dad, are sending their children the wrong message. And it is a well-known fact that parents who allow their children to make their own decisions at an early age are setting themselves up for failure and humiliation as parents. Do you remember little Tommy's mother in the supermarket.

Many in today's society are paying the price for the neglect of parental guidance and discipline in the raising of children over the past 40 years. And because of this neglect, we live in an overly permissive society, where its okay to use the most vulgar language in television and radio programming without restraint.

And we really know that society has declined when people can proudly display "Four-letter-words" on the rear windows of the vehicles and on their bumpers, without shame or embarrassment. And how is a parent to answer the question from their kindergartener, or first-grader when asked the question, "what is that word on the back of that car, Mommy?'

Now, what about the hundreds and thousands of young people who are removed from our society and placed behind bars. Now why are they incarcerated? Even though many of them came from loving and nurturing homes, they are there because their wrong choices placed them in their present situation.

And what about children who grew up in wealthy families? A child can grow up in a wealthy family with a half-million dollar home and from all outward appearances, look normal and happy. But just like any middle-to-lower class family, there can be problems.

Now, in the case of middle class families with child discipline problems, some of those parents are so busy with other activities that they barely have time to actually sit down to eat with, nor have any physical contact with their children.

Since they are so busy, they never even bother to ask what their children are thinking, or feeling. And on top of that equation, many of those families have shattered marriages that stem from adultery and divorce, and their children are caught right in the middle of the whole fight.

And what happens to these children? Being a by-product of this overly permissive society, and a degree of parental neglect, they grow up having very low self-esteem, little or no self-restraint, and no self-discipline. So, the only place that brings them any semblance of order, structure, and discipline is jail, or prison, where guidance and discipline is not an option, but a requirement.

So, what happens to the juveniles who commit serious violent crimes? It is a very unfortunate circumstance, but they must suffer the consequences of their actions, and and they must go to jail. It has to be acknowledged that there are no current rehabilitation programs for criminal juvenile delinquents who are incarcerated in institutions that have a success rate that even approaches 50-percent. But, a program with a 20-percent success rate is considered extraordinary, even though they have an overwhelming number of failures.

It is also an unfortunate fact of life that the best place for some juveniles guilty of serious or violent crimes is jail, because that structured environment is the only place that seems to keep them under some kind of control.

Now, most people may not be aware that there is a modern urban challenge in today's society. The U.S. Census (2005 American Community Survey Nevada Corrections Department) stated that "just in the state of Nevada there were approximately 91,503 White households with both parents, and 19,979 where there was only a female head of household, and both categories of households had children under 18 years of age."

Among Black households, there were "approximately 22,735 with both parents and 12,739 of those households had only a female head of household, and those households had children under the age of 18."

In the Hispanic households with both parents, there were "approximately 63,070, with 12,687 homes with a female head, only, and both categories had children the age of 18.

And among Asian households, there were approximately 14,286 homes with both parents, with about 2,327 homes with only female heads, and both categories had children under the age of 18." Now, out of the same 2005 survey of Nevada households, there were 26,653 White males unemployed, and 5,609 in prison.

There were 4,903 Black males unemployed and 2,873 in prison. Among Hispanic households, there were 8.492 males unemployed, and 1,791 in prison. And among Asian males there were 2,366 unemployed, and 221 in prison. Native American statistics were unavailable because the sample cases were too small.

As we relate statistics, the question is, why was this a problem? The only answer that can be given depends upon the types of values that the parents have instilled in their children. Now, we can rest assured that the majority of these families are raising up their children with the core values of knowing the difference between right and wrong, but for those who make the wrong choices, there is a price to pay.

I find it an awful shame to see children as young as 13 years old being sentenced for life without parole for adult crimes. Joe Sullivan, a Black male was sentenced to die in prison in Florida, at 13 years of age, for sexual assault. There was also 14 year-old Evan Miller, Caucasian male who was sentenced to Life Without Parole in Lawrence County, Alabama 4 years ago. Antonio Russell, a Black male, was condemned to die in prison in Alabama at 15 years of age. And Omer Ninham, a 14-year-old Native American male was sentenced to die in prison in Wisconsin.

It has been reported by the news media, that over 2500 teens between 13 and 17 years of age have been sentenced to Life Without Parole in adult prisons across the United States. And another 74 documented cases where children under 14 years of age, or younger, have been issued the death penalty.

Now, the opponents of the issue of young teens in prison for life make claims that most of the children who have been sentenced to die in prison for crimes committed at thirteen and fourteen years old come from violent and dysfunctional backgrounds.

They also claim that they have been physically and sexually abused, neglected, and abandoned whose parents are prostitutes, drug addicts, alcoholics, and crack dealers.

They claim that these children grew up in lethally violent, extremely poor areas where health and safety were luxuries their families could not afford. And by the way, what are those institutions called, that are holding those young criminals who are being incarcerated at an alarming rate? Those institutions are called "Correctional Institutions."

So can they blame no else one but themselves, for the present situation that they find themselves in?

But there has been an update on the subject of juveniles serving life without parole. According to an article by Lilliana Segura in AlterNet, dated May 18, 2010, She stated that "the

U.S. Supreme Court has given a second chance to juveniles serving life without parole for non-homicide crimes."

She goes on to say that, "Children who commit crimes other than murder can no longer face a sentence of life without parole, the U.S. Supreme Court ruled Monday, in a highly anticipated decision that civil rights lawyer Bryan called "an incredibly important win for kids who've been condemned to die in prison without parole."

According to the article, "Justice Anthony Kennedy drew a parallel between the death penalty and life without parole, noting that while it is true that a death sentence is unique in its severity and irrevocability, life without parole sentences share some characteristics with death sentences that are shared by no other sentences."

Now, as previously stated, one of the main problems in our society, is that some parents want to be "best friends" with their children rather than face the difficult and responsible role as parents. This very loose and liberal approach to parenting has caused a world of problems in many families in America as well as a host of other countries.

If you don't believe me, ask some of the parents who have allowed this practice, and also ask them how easy is it to correct, discipline, or say no to that child who is treated as their best friend?

The root of the problem in so many households, is that the parents are either too lax, with no discipline in the family, or too strict and harsh with their children. And the children of the parents who are over-lax, or over-strict will most likely get into trouble.

Many children possess a deep desire to live in a "structured" household where there are set limitations and boundaries for them to follow. And believe me, if you as parents, don't set limitations and boundaries for your children right from the start, and enforce them, your children will be following the rules set by your local "correctional" institution at a future date, then it will be too late for them.

Now, please keep in mind, that there is no one-size-fits-all guide to parenting and discipline. But the ultimate goal for parents should be to raise their children to be mature and productive members of society. And along with their God-given parental role, is the responsibility of the parents to apply moral guidelines and disciplinary strategies, which every newly married couple should negotiate with each other, prior to having children.

Now, these disciplinary strategies may include times outs, grounding, removing of privileges, or even spanking, as a last resort, if and only if, all other "corrective measures" have been exhausted, and behavior has not improved.

There was a survey of more than 1,500 parents in 27 states, Canada, and Puerto Rico recently conducted by the Pediatric Academic Societies in 2005, which gave a "behind-closed-doors" look at how parents discipline their children.

In this survey, parents responded to the form of discipline most used by them and the results are as follows: "Time-outs:

42%; Removing privileges: 41%; Yelling: 13%; and Spanking: 9%; Sending to bedroom: 27%."

This survey was given to parents of children aged between 2 and 11 before the children's "well child" doctor visits. According to this survey, punishments were often tailored to the child's age.

Time-outs and spanking were reported more often for disciplining little kids aged 2-5, and older children were more likely to get privileges removed, be yelled at, or hear the old classic line, "Go to your room!"

Now, according to the article, "many parents are following in their parent's footsteps." In the survey, "many parents were asked to recall the discipline strategies their mothers and fathers used on them in childhood. Their answers mirrored their own methods. That is, parents tended to duplicate the type of child discipline they received from their own parents."

Shari Barkin, MD, one of the survey researchers of Brenner Children's Hospital, part of Wake Forest University Baptist Medical Center in Winston-Salem, North Carolina, stated that "the only form of parental discipline experienced in childhood that was not significantly associated with the current choice of discipline was spanking." And this survey showed that "children often grow up to practice the same methods of discipline that were used on them." This again proves why it is so important for parents to discuss and agree on disciplinary strategies with each other prior to having children so that there can be a team effort, and a sense of direction that can guide them in the sometimes difficult art of parenting.

Do you recall the dilemma of little Tommy's mother in the opening pages of this book? She was once told that if she spanked her erring child she could be arrested for child abuse. What is not correctly understood by most people, is the law concerning the use of spanking as a form of discipline.

I spent quite a bit of time researching state statutes and found some interesting facts concerning spanking, or corporal punishment. It is a fact that it is legal in all 50 states for a parent to spank, hit, paddle, whip, or otherwise inflict punitive pain on a child, insofar as the corporal punishment does not meet the individual state's definition of "child abuse."

A few years ago, the Oklahoma State Legislature amended their child abuse laws with a bill that "explicitly granted parents the right to use paddles, and switches to spank their children." The Bill was enacted reportedly in response to the Columbine High School killings in Littleton, Colorado, and to broaden the rights Oklahoma parents already had to spank their children under current laws.

My state of Nevada passed a similar Bill. And the law in the state of Alaska states that, " the parent/guardian may use reasonable and appropriate physical force upon the minor when, and to the extent, reasonably necessary and appropriate to maintain discipline." (Sec.11.81.430.[Cr.]

Now, Georgia's spanking law states that "physical forms of discipline may be used as long as there is no physical injury to the child. Sec. 19-7-5/19-15-1/49-5-180.[Ci.] Parent or person in loco parentis reasonably disciplining of a minor has no justification for a criminal prosecution based on that conduct." Sec. 16-3-20.[Ci.]

The state of Michigan's spanking law states that "parent/guardian/other person permitted by law, can reasonably discipline a child, including the use of reasonable force." Sec. 750.136b.[Cr.] The state of Arkansas specifically defines in its law the difference between "spanking", and "child abuse," by stating that, "abuse does not include physical discipline of a child if reasonable and moderate, and inflicted by a parent or guardian for restraining or correcting a child."

"Listed as not reasonable, or moderate for correcting or restraining is throwing, kicking, burning, biting, cutting, striking with a closed fist; shaking a child under 3; striking, or other actions which result in any non-accidential injury to a child less than 18 months; interfering with a child's breathing; threatening a child with a deadly weapon; striking a child in the face, or any other act that is likely to cause bodily harm greater than transient pain or minor temporary marks."

"[The statute states this as an illustrative, and not an exclusive list.] age, size, and condition of the child, and their location of the injury and frequency or recurrence of injuries shall be considered in determining "reasonable" or "moderate. "[Sec. 9-27-303(B).[Ci.] Parent/teacher/guardian/other care and supervision of a minor may use "reasonable" and "appropriate" physical force when, and to the extent, reasonably necessary to maintain discipline or promote the welfare of the child. As the statute continues, If the belief that the force is necessary is a reckless or negligent belief, then the above offers no defense to a crime if the culpability of that crime is proven by showing recklessness or negligence." Justification is not available if the person recklessly or negligently injured, or created a substantial risk of injury to a person." [Sec.5-2-614.[Cr.]

As previously stated, some of the 50 states begin the law with what abuse is, then specifies what abuse is not. Texas law concerning corporal punishment states that, "abuse does not include "reasonable" discipline by a parent/guardian/managing or possesory conservator if child is not exposed to substantial risk of harm." Family Code Sec. 261001.[Ci.]

It goes on to state that, "a parent/stepparent/parent/person standing in loco parentis (in place of parent) to child is justified to use non-deadly force against a child under 18 years of age, when, and to the degree the actor reasonably believes necessary to discipline, or safeguard, or promote child's welfare." Penal Sec. 9.61 [Cr.] Civil Code.

Now, I could list the entire 50 states and their statutes concerning spanking and corporal punishment, but that would be very time consuming as well as very boring to the reader, but the statutes I listed was to prove that the laws of the land are on the side of parental rights when it comes to discipline and their children and stands on the side of children when it comes to child abuse against them.

I will only list one more state statute concerning spanking for "good measure."

The state of Utah's corporal punishment statute is very simple, which states, "Force is justified, if used for reasonable discipline of a minor by parent/guardian/person standing loco parentis." Sec. 76-2-401.[Cr. So, I ask the question. Where, in any of these state statutes that are listed, do you find a prohibition against spanking a child for purposes of correction and discipline? And I also found that in 1997, a survey pointed out that 65 percent of Americans approved spanking, and not much less than 75 percent who did so in 1946.

Now, even though the state of California, along with all the rest of the United States have laws on the books approving the spanking of children as a form of discipline, it has been reported by the news media that California Assemblywoman Sally Lieber, a Democrat representing Mountain View, California, planned to give California parents a lesson in parenting, whether they like it or not.

She announced on January 25, 2007 that she would introduce a bill that would outlaw the spanking of children under the age of four years old by their parents. She seemed to believe that banning spanking in such a way is the logical continuation of laws that banned slavery, and protected women from being beaten by their husbands.

It is said that under the new law, if passed, parents caught spanking their child could face up to one year in jail, or a $1,000 dollar fine. Many believed that this bill would run out of gas, because there have been similar bills attempted before in California, Massachusetts, and Wisconsin, and have failed amid criticism that they would be unenforceable. This bill did go down in flames.

Now, such nonsense bids a question to be asked. Are people so insecure in their ability as parents, that they would have the state government take over their parenting role of disciplining their children?

This action by the Assembly Speaker Pro Tem had caused such a public reaction by her announcement, that she was swamped with requests for national media interviews, according to her staff. But of course, there were supporters who agreed with her, and were promoting the notion that a slap on the rear of children could cause irreparable harm to them.

I might also add the fact that because parents have been so negligent in the area of parental guidance and discipline, there are 22 states that have re-introduced corporal punishment in the public school system after being banned in most states, and state law allows those teachers and administrators to paddle children in order to maintain classroom discipline.

The list of 22 states where corporal punishment is legal are Alabama, Arizona, Arkansas, Colorado, Florida, Georgia, Idaho, Indiana, Kansas, Kentucky, Louisiana Missouri, Mississippi, New Mexico, North Carolina, Ohio, Oklahoma, Pennsylvania, South Carolina, Tennessee, Texas, and Wyoming.

Now, concerning corporal punishment in schools, it was reported that in the 2006-2007 school year, an overall 233,190 school children in the United States were subjected to physical punishment. And this was a significant drop of almost 18%, and continuing a steady trend from the early 1980's.

It must also be said that even though corporal punishment is permitted in schools by law in 22 of the 50 states, there are a list of nine regulations that are required in order to administer corporal punishment.

Those regulations are listed as follows: (1) Corporal punishment must be done in a fair, reasonable, and impartial manner. (2) Student must be forewarned that a specific behavior will result in corporal punishment. (3) Student must be given opportunity to explain his or her actions. (4) Corporal punishment must be administered in the company of professional staff member notified beforehand. (5) It must be used only after other punishments have failed.(6) Procedures specified do not apply if the behavior is so blatant, disruptive, anti-social, or flagrant in nature as to shock the conscience.

(7) Teachers and principals must keep written records specifying when and why the punishment was administered. (8) If parents request a copy of written explanation, the principal must provide it. (9) Principals must hold each member of

his staff accountable for understanding the regulations and administering corporal punishment.

Now, at some of these schools, parents have the option of forbidding the use of corporal punishment, but very few parents ever do. In order to show how important learning, order and discipline is to school administrators, I found that states such as Alabama, Arkansas, Colorado, and Texas, along with four other states provide teachers immunity from civil and criminal prosecution for using corporal punishment, and order other school systems to provide legal support, as well as support in pressing criminal charges against any student who might attack a teacher.

It is interesting to find in my research, that many outside of the United States have a different attitude about spanking than those inside the U.S. The Arkansas Democrat-Gazette posted a story concerning corporal punishment on May 30, 1997,

With the heading, "Denmark law bans parents spanking kids." The article stated that, "Denmark joined its Nordic neighbors Wednesday in prohibiting parents from spanking their children, or using other kinds of corporal punishment.

After a heated debate in the parliament, the spanking ban squeaked by in a 51-54 vote. Opponents contended that the measure was too intrusive on the family by the government. Tove Fergo, a member of the Liberal Party said that "the law would "criminalize" parents using normal methods to raise their children."

At this present time, there are six nations, besides Denmark, that have banned spanking as a form of discipline in families. Those countries are Norway, Finland Sweden, Austria, Cyprus, and Italy.

It is a known fact that no government can fill the role of the parent, no matter hard they try. And experience has shown, that even though they may mean well, the government, in any country, is a wildly expensive and lousy substitute parent.

So, instead of allowing the state or federal government to act as substitute parents for your children, "you," as parents, need to step up to the plate, and take aggressive measures to maintain your parental, emotional, and financial responsibilities as you have been given a "God-given" right.

Now, we as parents or grandparents must understand, that if there is little or no guidance or discipline in the home, most children will draw the conclusion that they can do as they please and this sends a signal to the child that their parents don't really love or care about them, or what they do. And this neglect that we see on the part of many young parents is learned behavior which is, without a doubt, passed down from generation to generation.

And this only adds to the generational vicious cycle of parental neglect. And these types of home situations can also lead to child abuse in the family. Now, why do I say these things? I say this because in a "free spirit" type of family situation, the only true communication that some parents have with their children is to punish them when they get into trouble, either at school or with law enforcement officials.

And those parents who are angry at their children will attempt to punish them while in a "fit of rage. And if a parent disciplines a child in a fit of frustration, anger and rage, the end result will more than likely be child abuse.

Now, when it comes to parental discipline, there has to be a balance for discipline to work correctly. The question that comes to mind is, what is discipline, and what is its ultimate purpose?

According the Encarta World English Dictionary [North American Edition] MSN 2007, there are seven definitions concerning discipline listed there, and I will list all seven of them. They read as follows: (1) Training to ensure proper behavior; the practice, or methods or teaching and enforcing acceptable patterns of behavior. (2) Order and Control; a controlled orderly state, especially in a class of school children. (3) Calm Controlled behavior; the ability to behave in a controlled and calm way even in a difficult, or stressful situation.

(4) Conscious control over lifestyle; mental self-control used in directing, or changing behavior; learning something or training for something. (5) Education Activity; or subject or field of activity, ie, an academic subject. (6) Punishment designed to teach somebody obedience. (7) Christianity church rules; the system of rules used in a religious denomination or order.

It must be understood that there is no "one-size-fits-all" disciplinary technique. On one extreme, a parent can be over-permissive excusing all of their child's misbehavior as normal for a child. And on the other hand there could be a serious case of over-discipline in which a parent acts like a tyrant, not allowing the child to make any mistakes.

And those types of parents show very little love to their children, and constantly administer harsh discipline at all times.

So, there must be an even balance between "over permissiveness", and the "over-disciplining" of children.

But it is up to parents to decide what is necessary and reasonable discipline for their children. And whatever method of discipline and teaching techniques they choose, if spanking is included as one of the forms of discipline, it is very important that it that always be used as a last resort after all other corrective measures have been exhausted, in resolving the issue at hand.

Now, even though abuse of children does occur in single, as well as two parent families, it also occurs in homes where there is drug use, alcoholism, and divorce. And unfortunately, the children are caught right in center of it all.

Now, in many instances, a divorced parent brings in a "live in" boyfriend, or a "live in" girlfriend, and either situation places any children in the family at a high risk for abuse. Especially when the children are left in the care of either "live in" partner.

It is not hard to understand, how a little child like 4-year-old Tommy, is allowed to be out-of control in a supermarket with out restraint. And if a child like the 5-year-old boy on the "Nanny 911" television program is allowed to hit his mother in the face and curse at her on a world-wide television program, what will happen when little ones like these become teenagers in that family?

If anyone in America watches television news, reads the newspaper, listens to the radio, or gets their news from the internet, they will see, or hear about children like Tommy in their teens participating in gang violence, committing murder in schools, and out-of-control across the country.

Now, the questions is, who is responsible for the aberrant actions of these out-of-control teens? Everyone shrugs their shoulders and scratches their heads as they try to find an answer to that question.

But if anyone knows state law across the United States, parents are held accountable, for the actions of their children from the time that they are born, until they reach eighteen years of age. And state law assures parents the right to discipline their children, mainly because law enforcement officers and state authorities have to deal with these young people in the juvenile justice system every day.

As we live and breathe, it is not hard to see, that many parents are afraid of their children. An incident comes to mind, where a mother told her son to stop bouncing his basketball against the side of the house because the ball was breaking the side paneling.

Angry for being told to stop what he was doing, the young teenager started swearing at his mother and told her to shut up, and go away. Without saying another word his mother simply turned around and went back into the house.

Now, if parents are having quite a bit of difficulty controlling their teenage children, how about others who have contact with them, such as teachers, who have the responsibility of instructing millions of these young people on a daily basis around the world.

Now, please keep in mind, that we are talking about a small percentage of "underachievers" who need a large "dose of discipline." But there are a larger percentage of parents who deserve recognition for carrying out their God-given duty to raise responsible and upstanding children to adulthood.

But one of the problems in the school systems across the country is that teachers are limited in their ability to teach, because so much time is being spent correcting students for misconduct in the classroom.

And when these errant students are dealt with, and punished at school, many parents take the side of their children against the teachers and school administrators, rather than attempt to hold their young troublemakers accountable for their actions. And it is a well-known fact that children who are not disciplined in the home, are destined for trouble outside the home.

So teachers, school administrators, and fellow students end up becoming the ultimate targets of unimaginable violence. We must realize the fact that schools all over America and abroad, are being overcome by violence, and the only solution to the problem is to get to the root cause, and deal with it swiftly and directly.

Now, because of such a high degree of violence in the school systems across America, I read an article from Associated Press, dated July, 2010, that a Detroit-area prosecutor wanted lawmakers to pass an ordinance that could jail parents for up to three days for repeatedly missing scheduled parent-teacher conferences."

It was stated that "Wayne County Prosecutor Kym Worth said that such an ordinance was aimed at making parents responsible for their children's education, which may keep more young people out of trouble."

Everyone should know that school violence does not just begin there, but directly flows from adverse situations in the home life. The lack of parental limitations and boundaries for children in the home, and the overindulgence of their parents giving in to every whim can be ingredients for disaster.

Now, what are some of the violent acts unleashed by many of those undisciplined children and youth? Many of them participate in acts of aggression towards people, such as bullying, fighting, mugging, and sexual crimes using guns, knives, and other weapons.

These troubled kids are also the root cause behind much destruction of property, including tagging, arson, and other damage. Now, if parents would follow through with their parental responsibilities, they would notice changes in the attitudes and behaviors of their children. And serious indicators that there are problems with these children include violations of house rules such as staying out late at night without permission; exhibiting a lack of interest in school; an epidemic of failing grades; as well as dropping out of school.

So, if parents don't know what their children are doing from day to day, that can lead to a world of problems. Do you recall the massacre at Columbine High School, where two teenage male students carried out a shooting rampage, killing twelve fellow students and a teacher, as well as wounding 24 others, before committing suicide. And as the investigation of that horrific tragedy began to unfold, it was found, that those two young teens wrapped themselves around the gothic sub-culture; heavy-metal music; a heavy indulgence of pharmaceutical drugs; violent films; and violent video games.

Now, some people claim that video games are just games. So what is the problem with video games? The problem with video games is that even though they are just games, the simulated games involving shooting can teach some real skills about using weapons.

I hope that everyone is aware of the fact that any emotionally unstable person can very easily turn those simulated shooting skills onto real people. And in the process of playing video games where supposed enemies are killed, the players of the games become desensitized to the horror of real killing.

So, if this simulated killing ever does become real, it could be carried out with a complete lack of empathy for real victims. It must be understood, that if a person is predisposed to violence because of an inner hurt or anger; violent music, movies, or video games, this can combine to provide the catalyst and skills necessary to commit real crimes. And this combination of things can draw young minds away from what is good and right, and push them into the very threshold of the door to mayhem, death and destruction.

Now, the question comes to mind. Where were the parents in the lives of those young murderers at Columbine High School, and what could they have done to prevent such a horrible tragedy by their sons?

Could they have possibly returned the phone calls from the teachers, and school administrators who dealt with their sons on a daily basis? Could they have possibly been more involved in knowing who their sons friends were, and what kind of things they participated in with their friends? And could they have possibly been more observant of the actions and attitudes of their sons?

Now, as we have been made aware of things that have lead up to young people committing horrible and vicious crimes of murder in schools across the country, in the last 10 to 15 years, it leads me to focus on some possible preventative measures that parents can take to never have this happen to their child.

Would it hurt for them to conduct weekly inspections of their teen's bedrooms to see what kind of music they are listening to, or what kind of video games they are playing on a day-to-day basis. They might also check their internet websites visited, as well as Facebook, cell phone, and texting contacts periodically.

Now, what is wrong with checking under the beds and mattresses of the children, as well as their closets, to see if their are any weapons, or anything unusual that should not be there. And as a parent, you may be confronted by your teenager for going into their bedroom, claiming that they have a constitutional right to privacy?

If you been confronted by your child in such a manner, the news should be flashed to the mind of your young complainer, that as long as he is still under your roof, their bedroom is "subject to search."

Now, it seems that there had not been much attention given to the unbelievable amount of senseless murders and carnage by children until Columbine, but there have been over 44 such episodes since the early 1990's.

I will attempt to list a few of them. On February 2, 1996 there was the murder of two students; one teacher and another wounded when a 14 year-old male student opened fire in his algebra class at Moses Lake, Washington. Could this horrendous crime have been prevented?

On February 19, 1997, a high school principal, and one student were killed, and two others were wounded by a 16 year-old in Bethel, Alaska. On October 1, 1997 two students were killed and seven were wounded by a 16 year-old in Pearl, Mississippi. And that same teenager killed his mother before going to school that day.

Now, two months after the school shooting in Mississippi, three students were killed, and five wounded on December 1, 1997 by a 14 year-old male student as his victims participated in a prayer circle at Heath High School, in West Paducah, Kentucky. And it wasn't fifteen days later on December 15, 1997, that a 14 year-old male student killed two students who were standing in the school parking lot in Stamps, Arkansas.

Such examples of school shootings and murders by children and teenagers have plagued this nation, and other countries from late 1990 on through to 2008. And I could list many more of these horrible crimes, but I am sure that you get the point that I am trying to make.

Now, it grieves my heart, as I think about the hundreds of innocent people who were wounded or killed at the hands of so many of those young twisted individuals, as well the family members who are still mourning the loss of their loved ones even to this day. But I have heard many people in all walks of life ask this one question. Why? Why did these young murderers do such a thing?

Now, I grant you, if the parents of these twisted individuals would have carried out their God-given responsibilities to love, nurture, guide, and discipline their children from infancy to eighteen years of age, they could have possibly prevented such horrendous carnage at the hands of their children.

It was lamented by some people, that this situation with school shootings may not ever be 100% resolved, and may have to be accepted as a normal part of our society. On that notion, I disagree.

The message that I have been sharing, and will continue to share, is that unless parents do their part in setting limitations and boundaries in the family regarding their children, reigning in their errant habits and tendencies through disciplinary and corrective measures as soon as they arise these types of tragedies will continue to occur.

Now, many thought leaders have suggested that teachers and school administrators be allowed to arm themselves with guns so that any future perpetrators could be stopped while carrying out plans of terror, murder and mayhem. And, I do believe that if would-be murderers knew that their would-be victims possessed weapons to fight back, that would cause them to stop and think a little bit more about the consequences of their actions.

But, it is just the same as the bank robber who knows that there are armed security guards, and cameras in the bank, but they still continue to rob banks nevertheless. So, it all goes back to the same issue.

If parents would teach their children the difference between right and wrong and correct them when there behavior is unacceptable, they could possibly prevent their children from hurting themselves and others. So, how is it possible for parents to help prevent such carnage? Some of the possible ways is for parents to stop fighting school teachers and administrators in their desire to promote school safety; improve discipline problems; and allow children to learn without being fearful of being bullied or killed at school by those who don't want to be in school in the first place.

Most people would agree that the first priority of a good school system is to have a safe, secure, and disciplined environment where learning is the key focus.

And that goal cannot be accomplished unless parents agree to allow their school districts across the nation to implement school uniforms for each and every student, in all grades. But why school uniforms?

In response to growing levels of school violence in our schools, many parents, teachers, and school administrators have come to see school uniforms as one way to improve discipline and school safety.

Now, why would some parents fight such a positive measure? Some parents seem to feel that their children should be able to express their individuality in the way that they see fit. But isn't that just the attitude that is going on in the schools right now, as schools across the nation have become literal "killing fields"

Are you aware that many school officials across the country have observed that the adoption of school uniform policies enhances the learning environment, and increases school safety at the same time.

In these observations they have found that there has been decreasing violence and thefts among students, especially over designer clothing and expensive athletic footwear.

A school uniform policy also helps to prevent gang members from wearing gang colors, and insignia at school, as well as eliminates the "sagging pants" syndrome that so many school officials have to combat every day. It also helps to instill within students the comfort of a disciplined and structured environment.

It is key in helping students resist peer pressure; to stay focused in the classroom, and makes it possible for school officials to recognize any young people who are not authorized on school property.

Now, if those parents who are opposed to school uniform policies are concerned about the education and safety of their children, they should take the time to research the positive results that have been gained by the use of such policies in the states that have installed them, and encourage their local school boards to implement those policies as soon as possible, because the very education and lives of their children are at stake.

It has been reported that the following states have adopted school uniform regulations, And they are listed as: California, Florida, Georgia, Indiana, Louisiana, Maryland, New York, Tennessee, Utah, and Virginia.

Now, it is also interesting to note that the following large city public school systems have enacted either voluntary, or mandatory uniform policies and they are: Baltimore, Cincinnati, Dayton, Detroit, Los Angeles, Long Beach, Miami, Memphis, Milwaukee, Nashville, New Orleans, Phoenix, Seattle, and St Louis. The School uniform regulations in those cities were mostly in elementary and middle schools.

Now, the school boards and administrators in those states and cities must be commended for their courage to stand up to much opposition, in either enforcing school dress codes that were already in place, as well as for implementing stringent school uniform policies that will help to provide a safe and secure learning environment that will pay off when it is all said and done. As we spoke earlier about crime and the criminal element, there is a segment of our society that is estimated at close to one million members.

That segment, believe it or not, is the number of children and teens that are in street gangs across America. besides being extremely loyal to each other, many of them feel closer to one another, than their own family members.

Now, I don't know about you, but I cannot understand why any adolescent or teenager in their right mind would want to join a gang whose main activities are terrorizing neighborhoods, breaking into homes; carjacking; selling drugs; participating in random acts of violence and drive-by shootings on a daily basis, and seemingly doing whatever they desire simply because they want to.

Some of these young people may simply join gangs for protection. If there is a bully on school grounds, some of the weaker children may find help from gangs to protect them.

Peer pressure is another reason that youth connect with gangs and fear plays a a tremendous part in it. Now, do you think that youth join gangs because they enjoy being humiliated, and nearly beaten to death by other gang members during initiation. If this is the case, there is something terribly wrong with our society.

Now, a point to be considered, is that perhaps these youth join gangs because they receive little or no love, or meaningful interaction at home, and in their mindset, they are feeling that at least they can get some semblance of love, attention, and even discipline from their supposed adopted family of gang leaders, and fellow members. According to the American Civil Liberties Union, an estimated 270,000 guns are taken to school in the United States every day. And young people, whether in or out of gangs knows that guns are present, and many students try their best to keep away from these types of people.

And for many others who find it very difficult to avoid the relentless harassment by gang members have one of two choices. They can either give in and join, or quit school. And that is a great problem that we have in our present day society.

Now, many parents have attended the funerals of their young people ranging from as young as twelve to the age of eighteen-years-old. It is very unfortunate, that many young lives have been snuffed out because of the wrong choices that they made.

But I believe that those senseless deaths could have been avoided if their home situations had been better.

Now, I am not totally blaming all parents for this problem, because most parents have tried very hard to be involved in the everyday lives of their children. And many parents are working more than one job to make ends meet. But some of these parents could have made better choices in the raising of their children, and their relationships with them.

Today's parents need to spend more "quality time" with their children and one of the ways of doing this is at the dinner table. Family time at the dinner table has become a rarity, especially because of parents' differing work schedules. So, setting limits and boundaries for your children; having meaningful conversations with them; and letting them know that you care about them, can go a long way.

Simply throwing a little money at your children, and sending them to the mall, or movies, is just not enough for them. Parents, your children need you. Your children deserve more than that.

And a measure of family structure, discipline, and order can make a world of difference in the lives of children, because that is what true parenting is all about. It must be made very clear to your children that if they make a mistake, you will correct them but continue to love them. But if your child knowingly commits a criminal act they can be absolutely sure that the consequences for their actions will follow close behind.

So, what should parents do? Parents should be more proactive with their children, and spend more time with them. More than just hello, and goodbye. If your children are "telling" you where they are going, rather than "asking" you for permission to go, you have a problem.

Now if the only time you see your kids is when they get up in the morning to go to school, and at night before they go to bed, you have a problem. If you don't know what your children are wearing to school every day, you have a problem. And if "you", as a parent, are not watching for signs of unusual behavior in your children, and talk to them about it before it escalates into a potentially uncontrollable situation, you have a problem.

Now, don't forget, "you" are the parents. And as parents, "you" are responsible. in most states, for the actions of "your" children. And whether 'you" chose the time to give then birth, or not, they are legally under "your" care from infancy to adulthood. So, stand up, and be counted. And be responsible parents. Guide your children in the right direction. Provide a safe home environment for them, where they can learn, grow, and mature into productive, and responsible adults. And I might add that complete family involvement in a church and worship setting can greatly provide strength and support for your family unit. That is why there is an admonition to parents in the Bible, "Train up a child in the way he should go, and when he is old, he will not depart from it." (Proverbs 22:6) Therefore, the combination of genuine love, nurturing, training, and corrective discipline when needed, is the key for a safe home environment.

There has been much talk about poverty in the United States. It has been estimated that there are approximately 37 million people living below the poverty line in this country. And that includes more than 12.9 million children under the age of 18. How is that possible here in the U.S.? We would think this would only happen in third world countries. But it is indeed a reality here in the United States Of America. Now, how did we come to this unfortunate position?

We constantly hear the statistics such as 25% of New Yorkers are children, and 762,000 of them live in poverty in New York City alone. That means that there were approximately 181 babies born in poverty in New York City each day, and 10,000 children are homeless, and that number has doubled since 1988.

Now, on the other side of the country in the state of California, the number of children living in poverty has increased, and is significantly worse than the national average, according to an analysis of census data by Children's Defense Fund.

According to CDF's analysis, 17.7% of children nationally live in poverty, compared to 19% in California. And according to the National Center for Children in Poverty, the number of low-income children in California has increased by almost 1.6 million; from 2.77 million to 4.36 million. And the number of California's children in poverty has increased by 859,000; from 1.27 million to 2.12 million.

Now, I have a question. Where did all these children come from? Out of all these statistics, one thing that I don't hear, is that a great number of these children who are in poverty, are born to young mothers out of wedlock.

As I stated earlier in these pages, the lives of unwed mothers are very difficult. They are placed in a position of trying find a way to provide for themselves and their newborn child.

And since a great number of these young mothers are junior high, and high school students, they are left to depend greatly on their parents, grandparents, other relatives and friends, in order to survive. And this, for the most part, places an added burden on those family member who have already raised their own children to adulthood.

In most cases, for these young mothers, if there is little or no family support for them and their child, the only relief that they can find is to turn to government-supported programs, which provide billions of dollars in aide to poor families per year.

Now, I found in my research, that many of these young women not only turn to programs that provide food and shelter for them, but they also take advantage of other programs that can help them complete their high school education, either by attending night school for their high school diploma, or by working toward their GED.

Now, upon completion of high school, or GED, some of these young women seek programs such as "Pell Grants", to help them move toward a college education in order to improve their lives and make it better for their children.

Now, this was the main purpose for the "Welfare To Work" program initiated by the Republican led Congress, and signed by then President Bill Clinton in 1996, which dropped the welfare rolls from 5 million to 2 million unwed mothers. So as a result, 60% of the mothers who left welfare found meaningful employment.

These bold steps by single mothers with children, who were once in dire straights and on the poverty rolls, have become independent from welfare by going to work; improving their lives; increasing in self-esteem; and setting high setting standards for themselves by teaching their children not to make the same mistakes that placed them on the welfare rolls.

Now, I have thought about this poverty situation, and I have considered some things that might be helpful in resolving the blight on society amongst us. It has been said that the majority of the people in poverty are working, but are not making enough income to rise above the poverty line. Now, where are these people working and what kind of jobs are they holding?

Many of them are working at entry-level service jobs at fast-food restaurants. Maybe they are not aware of the fact that those types of entry-level jobs are not made for adults with a wife and two or three children, but geared more for teenagers who seek part-time work either for the summer, or after school, to earn spending money for themselves.

I would like to offer several solutions to the poverty dilemma, and they are listed as follows: For those who did not do very well in school and either barely graduated, or received a GED, there are trade-schools that provide training, in different fields such as nursing assistant; trucking driving; electronics; dental assistant; hotel-motel management; and many other areas that, once completed, can raise their income to well above the poverty and minimum wage levels.

So, if you know people who have been living in mediocrity; depending on the government for never-ending assistance; waiting for the next pittance to be given to them; let them know that if they really desire to rise above their present living conditions, they have the opportunity to take the challenge, believe, and achieve, seek out a trade school, and follow their dreams.

Now, they must always keep in mind, that success will not come overnight. It will take much patience, hard work, and determination.. And if they get out of the bed or off the couch, and work hard toward their goal, they will succeed and reap great benefits for their efforts. And if you doubt what I say, ask the ones who have done it and they will tell you that all that hard work was worth it.

It is important to remember, that failing to guide and discipline a child is a form of neglect and abuse. Some think that this type of abuse happens in only poor families, but it takes place in every walk of life, even of the wealthy.

Now, how many times have you heard parents say, "We gave that boy or girl everything they could ask for, and they repay us by getting into trouble, or ending up in jail." I assure you that most people may give their children everything they ask for, but those "things" are not enough!

It could be that the bad behavior, or the bad report card is an indication that your children are simply trying to get your attention by exhibiting such behavior. Remember the phrase, "Negative attention is better than no attention at all?"

It is sad to say, but that is the case in many families. There are children and youth in all walks of life, that are reaching out for some kind of response from their parents.

Whether it be a hug and kiss every day, or some kind of meaningful conversation or interaction with Mom and Dad. But unfortunately, the only time that there is any kind of interaction between some parents and children is in the Principal or Dean's office, after the parents are called to the school as a result their child's misbehavior in the classroom.

Now, there are some areas in family life that parents with children need to carefully examine. If your are parents who are too busy to communicate and interact with your children, you need to reorganize you lifestyle, and reset your priorities.

If you never take time to show affection to your children with a kiss, a hug, and a long conversation while sitting down at the dinner table with your child, there is a problem in your family.

If you never bother to ask your child how their day went at school, or what they are thinking or feeling, there is a problem in your family. If you take time out of your daily schedule to spend quality time with your children every day, you will not only show them that you really love and care about them, but you will be setting a pattern that will train your children to do the same for your future grandchildren when your children grow up, get married, and start their own family as well. The "special" time that you give your children is called nurturing, which should have begun at the birth of your child, and must continue on through to their adulthood.

Now, many children have come up with the idea that once they reach 12 to 16, they are old enough to make their own decisions and don't believe they need their parents' advice and consent on what they buy, what they wear, where they go, or what they do. But I believe that train of thought is dead wrong.

If you open your eyes wide and observe the teens in today's society, you will see a breakdown in the attitude and the lack of critical thinking of these kids. Where are they getting these ideas?

There is no doubt in my mind, that these kids are more than likely being influenced by the media venues of VH1, BET, MTV, and Teen magazines because they may not be receiving any guidance at home.

Now, what do these media venues offer to these young enquiring minds full of mush? Some of them deal with instructions on interpersonal relationships such as, what to wear, and what not to wear; what to eat and what not to eat; and some of these programs even promote the piercing and tattooing of their bodies in the programs they produce.

Even at the writing of these pages there are television shows that promote and advertise the (so called) art of tattooing and the wonderful advantages of it. Now, I cannot understand why a person would have the desire to go through the pain that comes with the mutilation of the skin unless they are sado-masohists.

But when we as parents really consider this subject, we don't realize how easy it is for us to sit in front of our televisions with our children and grandchildren to watch a great game of Basketball, Football, or some other sports program and here comes the subliminal messages from tattoo laden athletes to us. And that message is, "look at me, I have a tattoo. I don't know why I have actually have gone through the pain of getting it, but I just had to get one because it looks so good on me."

And because these young minds can so easily be influenced by these athletes and celebrities, and what they see on television, parents need to be aware of what their children view in this media, and act accordingly, or you will lose control of your children at a very early age.

Now, to see how far our society has gone down, we not only see tattoo-laden bodies resembling local city billboard, but we also see an abundance of noses, ears, eye brows, lips, and tongues laden with rings, studs, and assorted jewelry.

And could it be possible, that all of the pain received to the bodies of young and old on a daily basis be a symptom of deep-seated psychological problems, and is actually a negative means of crying out for love, attention, and acceptance but no one is listening?

Now, if by chance this is the case, should psychological testing be required by law, before anyone is permitted to receive tattoos, piercing, or any type of body modification? And in my opinion, any child under 18 years of age is not capable of making an informed decision, but is easily succumbed to "faddism."

And is this faddish form of self-expression through body modification actually safe? Now, there is some information concerning tattoos and piercings that is not readily made available for those seeking to modify various parts of their bodies in order to express themselves, and it is not good news.

Because tattooing and piercing both cut through the protective surface of the skin, they risk serious infection. Now, historically, tattoos have transmitted such pathogens as syphilis, staphylococcus, HIV, and Hepatitis B. And there is now a suspicion about Hepatitis C.

Now, parents should be aware, that the afore-mentioned Hepatitis viruses attack the liver, and could cause jaundice, fever, or even liver failure. And since the liver is the site of many biochemical reactions in the body, liver failure from cirrhosis can cause death, unless a liver transplant is available. So, it is incumbent upon parents, and young people contemplating such a procedure, to be aware of what this form of self-expression, or self-mutilation could lead to.

Now, another thing to consider, is that many tattoo wearers who received their body art before marriage and children, have come to regret that choice, and are now seeking ways to have their body art removed, and such a procedure can also be a painful, arduous, and expensive undertaking.

So, before going through the procedure of getting a tattoo, it is best to study the "pros" and "cons" and weigh all of the psychological, physiological, and assorted medical facts associated with it before getting it done, because the human body was not originally created to be a "canvass" for tattoo artists, nor a "pin cushion" for so-called body piercing professionals.

Now, anyone keeping up with current events heard the news report stating that 9 million children in America do not have health care. Now, the question that arose in my mind was, why are these nine million children living without healthcare? Are they living on their own without parents?

Or could it be, that their parents were not offered a health plan through their employment? Could it be that their parents chose not to buy into an HMO, or other health insurance program?

Or could it be that their parents decided to use the money which could have paid for health insurance on other things more important? Or could it be that the parents are unemployed and could not afford insurance at all. And as you know, many people have lost their jobs and are in a very desperate situation.

And any form of health insurance for many, is out of reach. Many of you are also aware that the National Healthcare Bill was recently passed by the Congress of the United States and was signed by President Obama. Now, no matter how it is sliced or diced, it is "government-run healthcare". And, there are diverse opinions as to whether it is good for America, or not.

But, one of the main reasons that health insurance has gone through the roof in America is because Congress refuses to lift the restrictions placed on the health insurance companies.

These restrictions block their ability to sell health insurance across state lines just as auto insurance is sold, which would increase competition and help to lower the cost of healthcare.

Now, I want to say that most people in this situation are aware that by state law, emergency rooms cannot deny treatment to anyone who walks through its doors even though they are unable to pay. But, some people believe that the state funded hospital services are all that they need, and they don't need any preventive health or dental care plan, even if they could afford it.

But, I want to say that my wife and I have been blessed by God to be able to earn a living by working hard every day, which affords us the opportunity to pay for a health, and dental insurance plan because we care about our health.

We also choose to pay for life insurance because it is very important to have for family security. But, we are also required by law to purchase auto insurance because to not do so would be in violation of the law.

So if we, and other parents choose to provide affordable health care for our families, what is the problem with some of those parents of the nine million children who don't have it, but can afford it. It involves a matter of life or death, and I believe that the choice for health care lies in the hands of the parents of those children and no one else. Especially the government.

Now, the following questions need to be answered by you, as parents. Do you love your children? Do you tell your children that you love them, every day? Do you know where your children are at all times? Do you know the names of your children's teachers and principal at school?

How much quality time do you spend with your children each day? Do you know the types of clothes your children wear to school? Do you know your children's friends by name? Do you allow your children to make their own decisions?

Is mutual respect between you and your children practiced in your household? Do you assign your children chores to do around the house? Do your children ever tell you that they hate you? Do you set ground rules for your children to follow, and do you follow up when rules are broken? Do you help your children with their homework?

How often do you eat at the dining room table with your children? Does your family take time to go to a place of worship at least once a week? Do you set curfew times for your children to be home at night?

Do your children ask can they go out, or do they tell you they they are going out? Now, Believe it or not, your children are looking to you for leadership, guidance, protection, consistency, patience, nurturing and love. And if you are not setting an example for them as parents, how are they ever going to learn how to be parents themselves, one day in the future? Their future is in your hands, and it begins with you today. This is the Bottom Line.